To Andrew,
Cherish every 8!
Hebrews 13:2

Coach D.

TO BE THE KING OF DIAMONDS

Walter Ryan Adams

Order this book online at www.trafford.com
or email orders@trafford.com

Most Trafford titles are also available at major online book retailers.

Printed in the United States of America.

ISBN: 978-1-4269-5635-5 (sc)
ISBN: 978-1-4269-5636-2 (hc)
ISBN: 978-1-4269-5430-6 (e)

Library of Congress Control Number: 2011901288

Trafford rev. 02/17/2011

 www.trafford.com

North America & international
toll-free: 1 888 232 4444 (USA & Canada)
phone: 250 383 6864 ♦ fax: 812 355 4082

Foreword

As any high school teacher would tell you, success is found in the classroom when your students begin to ask profound questions. Moreover, that success is heightened when the same students overcome obstacles and discover the answers. It has been called many things: 'the light bulb going on', maturation, or even enlightenment. However it is known, we tend to recognize it when we see it. Of the many paths taken to discovery, the best part is not the destination, it's the road taken. Forgive me for sounding 'Frost-like', but there is substance to this way of thinking. Each year that I teach in the classroom or coach on the field (as does every other idealist teacher/coach), I attempt to emphasize this point. In my effort to do this each year, at a particular date, I tell a story.

I have found that some of the greatest orators, the great teachers I have had, and the great coaches I have come to admire share a certain quality. They are able to tell a fantastic story. The stories that they tell are usually of certain incidents from their lives. These stories bring with them a valuable lesson to be learned. These recollections are meant to channel an understanding to be imprinted on the lives of the people that hear them. By recalling the details of our past we are, in turn, creating a moment. For moments we remember. It is by moments that we are defined.

I used to love cowboys and rodeo when I was a kid. My dad used to tell me that I would wake up in my crib in the middle of the night. The only thing that would calm me would be watching late night rodeo on the sports network. Of all the events, he said I would perk up most during the bull-riding. I think I enjoyed it because of the instant action that comes with the event. Bull-riders had merely 8 seconds to separate themselves from the rest.

The story that I tell revolves around moments of profound questions and even more profound answers; of a high school kid, a baseball, a speech, and a note. I make it a point to open the story the same way. I don't tell this story for me. I don't tell this story for them. I tell this story because I made a promise that I would never forget what happened. I would never forget what I learned. It is my story. It is my 8 seconds.

I

Could I ever wear the crown?

Throughout my life there have always been a few constants. No matter where I have been or where I ended up, the one thing that always seemed to remain was the game of baseball. I am currently a high school baseball coach and a teacher. I was never the best player. I was not born with the "five tools" to make it to the next level. I always described myself as a player who was good enough to play among the best but would not stand out as the best. Still, I believed early on that I was meant for something more. That belief carried me through my high school career and continues today. The game, in a way, saved my life. The game, in a way, gave me a life. I am forever in debt. This is one way I hope to repay that debt.

I was born and raised in Bogalusa, Louisiana. The city is located roughly seventy miles north of New Orleans. If Louisiana was a boot, my hometown would have been the big toe. Bogalusa used to be among the larger cities in the state. It was home to a paper mill and located in the pit of the racial tensions that plagued the South in the 1960s. When my parents graduated in 1969 and 1970 respectively, Bogalusa High School was being integrated. There were areas of the South that shared the struggles of integration. Bogalusa seemed to be one of the places that had yet to recover from those struggles. The population of my hometown went from around 30,000 residents when my parents were in their adolescence to nearly 13,000 during mine. As one can imagine, other aspects of the city also seemed to dissipate. Education and sports were two things that even I could notice at an early age.

Growing up in a Catholic family my parents recognized early that my sister and I would go to the local private school for our education. For high school it would be St. Paul's School located in Covington (some twenty-seven miles south of Bogalusa). From Kindergarten to my 7th or 8th grade year, though, I would attend Annunciation Catholic School. Annunciation was the same school that my mother and her seven siblings had attended. It was the same school my sister and cousins had attended. In fact, it was the same school in which my mother was my first grade teacher and my aunt was the principal. Needless to say, I never really got into trouble. I was in a comfort zone. It also helped that the class that I was in never grew beyond thirty students. It was easy, for the most part, to be accepted since the majority of that thirty had been together since preschool. We were on the same little league teams together, attending each others birthday parties, and certainly developed those long-lasting bonds that childhood friends seem to have. This is not to say that we are all the very best of friends to this day. Those bonds that developed were the kind where you can grow apart but still remember each other in those semi-embarrassing moments of childhood. It is this type of friendship that will become pertinent later in this story.

I was born in 1981, I loved sports (my parents used to tell me that "ball" was one of my first words), and I was asthmatic. My ailment put a few limitations on myself as a kid. Some of it I know was all in my head but I did have some legitimate reasoning. My Dad never wanted something like asthma to stop me. He wanted to provide me with all of the opportunities that he never received. Naturally, in every sport I played (attempted rather) Dad was our coach. Dad had the vision of his son one day playing in Bryant-Denny Stadium for his beloved Alabama Crimson Tide. It was a dream and I was a dreamer just as every seven year old seems to be. Football, then, would be our first obstacle and it was wasted on me early. When making through an entire game without having an asthma attack is an accomplishment, it may be time to find another sport. Furthermore, I did not take too much to the whole physicality of football. I was too soft. I tried Basketball in my preteen years. Thank goodness I had not done that before that time. That would have been asking for an attack. Also, I never took to the whole dribbling with your left hand thing.

Then there was Baseball. It was different. I liked the fact that you only had to run for a little while and get to stop at the next base. I liked the idea that if you hit the ball hard enough you could just jog around the bases. I liked the IDEA. I was not much of a home run hitter. In fact, I never hit one while in little league (not even in practice). But, regardless, I had found the sport that I would make my own. If my other classmates were to be good at all the other sports, then I had to be the best at this one. At least, that is the way I looked at it.

The trouble with your father trying to give you every opportunity is that it can be misconstrued by others. When you combine the small class size, the connections of my aunt as principal, my dad as coach, and myself as an overall asthmatically soft non-aggressive kid, there leaves little room for doubt that I was going to get picked on sometimes. It was obvious from my football background that I was not much of a fighter. So when I did get some riff from my friends, I let it get to me. By my sixth and seventh grade years, dad had put together an "all-star" team so we/I could play more games. I would hear from the other kids that the only reason I was on the team was my Dad was the coach. I felt that none of them thought I had any talent and for a while that is what drove me to play. I had to prove something. But as long as I was in Bogalusa that was not going to happen.

Our first "all-star" excursion followed a perfect 9-0 season during league play. The decision to not add any players from around the league (we thought) was the reason for our early dismissal from the famed 'Fire-cracker classic'. The next summer the best players from around the league were combined to form a team. The result was the same. In two summers we managed to win one game. We (our all-star team) were usually at the short end of ten run (sometimes twenty run) beat-downs. It was a reality check for us and a sign of the future of Bogalusa High School baseball. When the results from our games were frequently lopsided, it was difficult for there to be a significant passion for the game. Successful high school programs are developed from successful little leagues. "All-stars" had dropped baseball on the priority list for some of my teammates. It remained for me, though, among the top priorities.

Being on the teams that lost at such a frequent rate, I could not tell if I was any good. Without a basis for comparison, maybe the other kids were right. Maybe my passion for baseball was futile. Besides my dad, no one else really thought I was anything special. Maybe I was a delusional thinker. Maybe Dad and I both were. There was only way I could have found out. And I would.

4

At the end of seventh grade year, my parents sat me down to talk. They approached me with a simple question. Do you want to go back to Annunciation for your 8th grade year or do you want to go to St. Paul's? St. Paul's went from 8th grade to 12th. Those who went got a head start on high school courses and had a smoother transition to the overwhelming aspect of being a high school freshman. The choice was mine and it was a difficult one to make. If it had not been for one aspect of St. Paul's, the decision would have been a lot easier. I would have chosen to stay at ACS. I knew how my personality was and I knew the transition to such a large school would be almost too terrifying to handle. I did not want to leave my comfort zone… period.

I would not have been the only one going the next year (there was actually a small albeit significant population of Bogalusa students at St. Paul's) but I didn't care. That was until Dad brought up the one aspect, baseball. St. Paul's had an established baseball program that was among the best in the state. They had not won a state title before but they were always in the playoffs. The head coach was a man named Rick Mauldin who was known as a top tier baseball coach in Louisiana. If I went in 8th grade, I could make the 8th grade team and have my foot-in-the-door to play later on in high school. Then, since St. Paul's and Bogalusa High School were in the same district, I could play against some of my friends. It was a long shot because only one kid had ever made the varsity team at SPS and he rarely was in the lineup. Nevertheless, Dad knew how to help me make the "right" decision. If I wanted to find out how good I was, this was my best chance. I made the decision to attend St. Paul's in the fall of 1994 for my 8th grade year. Looking back, it was one of the best decisions that I have made.

To Be The King Of Diamonds

Its not always played on diamonds
Sometimes the field is rough
They said it wouldn't be that easy
But never told it to be this tough
I have been part of many teams
Made my home in different towns
Won and lost at many ballparks
And seen pitchers from different mounds
Lost some great teammates throughout my career
Met some more along the way
Had my share of slumps and errors
But was blessed enough to play
Sometimes I let the best pitch go bye
Now and again a homerun
Yet each day I prepare myself
For my moment in the sun
Sometimes I can help coach someone
Mostly I take advice
And it can be disheartening when ready to give it all
And you are asked to sacrifice
But could I ever leave my legacy?
Could I ever wear the crown?
To be the King of Diamonds
In my own Cooperstown
For it is not always how good you are
That makes one the best
It's the approach I bring to each at bat
That separates me from the rest
For I know in every season there are changes
And only two things do I claim
I play to go out a champion
And for the love of the game

July 2000

II

Lost some great teammates throughout my career

I am naturally a shy individual. So the first day I walked onto campus at St. Paul's, I was intimidated and overwhelmed by the size of the school and my class. I had not been apart of anything like it. St. Paul's is an all-boys Catholic school. This attribute had both positives and negatives. The negatives, for a teenage boy, were obvious. We did have a sister school just down the road from us so we were not completely void of the opposite sex, however, the setting of the high school made going to St. Paul's a unique experience. When you place thirteen and fourteen year old boys (all from various feeder schools) in this type of environment, the result, at least from my perspective, are the basics of social Darwinism. Each young man is out to establish himself as the alpha male or at least to be associated with the group of alphas. That was where my problem seemed to lie. In my experience as a high school teacher I have observed the similar patterns for any new kid that walks into unfamiliar hallways. They want to know, as I did, how to get involved in the right crowd;

how to find your niche and fit in. Standing out in a crowd was not my strong suit.

I remember for the first few months I had made up my mind as to how I was going to be known. I stayed rather quiet in class. I was not a complete introvert but I was not talking as much as I would have liked to have. I remember my parents mentioning to me that I should go out for the 8th grade football team. It would be a chance to get to know people and make friends. Given my history with shoulder pads, I didn't give playing much thought. Moreover, I didn't want to look stupid out there.

Sadly in my reasoning I would rather for guys not to develop an opinion of me whatsoever than to develop a bad one. There was one incident in particular that I remember. I went to one of the basketball games and was standing in the bathroom next to probably the best athlete in our class, Scott Dottolo. I remember conversing with him for a just a moment and in our passer-by exchange he referred to me as "Bo" at least twice. Briefly, I thought it was because I was from Bogalusa. I realized quickly that this was not the case. We had talked before (a couple of times before) and I was too nervous to even correct him and tell him that my name wasn't Bo, it was Ryan. I sat, instead, that semester envious of some of the popular kids like Scott. I would simply have to wait. I would have to wait for my constant. I would wait until baseball started in January. After all, it was the reason I had chosen to go to St. Paul's a year early anyway. Waiting, though, would mean maintaining the cocoon I had developed for a few more months.

In the first few months of my 8th grade year I did not like my decision that I had made. I was socially inept. I usually spent my weekends in the batting cage Dad had set up in the backyard. It was all that I knew. I once was told to keep in mind that there was always some other boy out there that was working harder than you were. That was part of what kept me in the cage seemingly all night. The other part can best be described as transference. I was unhappy and so I did the one thing that made me forget about things. It would rather ignite what I was trying to avoid. I would push myself until I would get upset with Dad. He would be hurt because he thought he was pushing me too hard. What was really happening was that I hit in the batting cage (practiced baseball) because I did not have the gumption to just be myself around my peers. Baseball was a crutch; my only crutch.

The first day of 8th grade tryouts had been marked on my calendar for months. There would be a two to three day evaluation to get the number of kids they wanted for the team. I think the anticipation outweighed my nervousness. I was ready to prove my doubters wrong. I knew I didn't have to be the best on the field. I just had to be in the upper percent. I was ready to get my foot in the door with my peers. I was ready to show what I could do. That was, until I saw the number of guys trying out. Sixty guys (at least) were trying out for eighteen spots.

It seemed every guy on the field was wearing an all-star jersey from the summer before. Of course, these were players on the same all-star teams that beat me and the boys from Bogalusa by a shade under three touchdowns. To make matters worse, I was trying out at second base with four other guys and right next to me was my ole' "Bo", the best athlete in the class of '99, Scott Dottolo. I just remember taking groundball after groundball. I honestly don't recall how well I did. My mind stayed focused on two things. One was on the superstar next to me whose glove seemed to be a magnet for every ball that came near him. The second thought was the, now, uneasy anticipation of getting to hit beside this guy tomorrow.

After the two and a half hours of evaluations we convened for the evening. Dad, of course, was anxiously awaiting my arrival in the car so we could discuss how the first day of tryouts went. When I got in the car Dad didn't hesitate, "*so...how did it go?*" All I could think to tell him was that I was competing for the same position as Scott Dottolo. He assured me that I probably did fine. That was what he was supposed to say. I was not as sure as he was.

The next day I recall walking to the lunch line outside of the cafeteria. The line had to be stopped outside to maintain crowd control. Hungry boys are hungry boys after all. As I stood in line I heard a voice say something behind me. It was Scott. When I turned around he looked at me as if meeting for the first time and said, "*Hey, you're Ryan Adams right*"? Because I was more curious about what was coming next I just assured him that I was. "*Man, you were awesome yesterday at second*". I think he noticed my mumbled "*huh*" sound and he continued, "*I just hope that I make the team now 'cause you didn't miss a thing...you have a lot of talent*". It took a moment for the previous phrases to register. I couldn't believe what I was hearing. Though he knows now, at the time, I do not think Scott Dottolo could have grasped then what those few words meant to me. It was so simple but carried so much more. The best athlete of our class, the popular kid, became the first person besides my father to ever tell me that I was any good. This certainly provided some added confidence for the remaining days of tryouts. It turns out that Mr. Dottolo and I were both correct in our observations. By the end of the week the final cuts had been made and both Scott and I made the 8th grade "A" team roster. I was now among the top of our class for the game of baseball and I owe in part to a few words spoken outside a cafeteria. I will never forget that moment.

I remember the first game we played was at Holy Cross High School in Chalmette. Scott started at second base. I, however, was the DH. I was becoming more comfortable. I wish I could say that all of my teammates were as accepting as Scott was but that would be false. We alternated time as designated hitter and second base throughout the season so we spent time together as we were sharing a position. He and I became friends. I was still not at the point where I hung out with the rest of the guys that Scott did but we had established a friendship nonetheless. For me, that was fine. I, at least, felt that by the end of my 8th grade year I had my foot in the door. I was more accepting of my choice to go to St. Paul's early and could not wait to be a freshman the next year. Baseball for the year, though, was not over. Because of our age, at fourteen years old all of us that played for St. Paul's were eligible to still play Little League. I, of course, played in Bogalusa for my father.

Being the only kid from Bogalusa to make the team at St. Paul's, I played all the Little League games as if I was the best player on the field. I may not have been but I still was able to "act as if". Instead of going the all-star route, Dad had organized a travel team for the summer. He wanted to make sure that I would get as many games in as possible. That summer (outside of a two week battle with viral meningitis) was going just as I had hoped. Dad had not seen me play like this before. It seemed that the hard work we put into those nights in the cage were paying off. I was playing with confidence; probably because I felt the possibilities that lied ahead for next year. Things were going smoothly. I even started to play third base instead of second. Eventually that would be where I had to move. In the plans for the future of St. Paul's baseball, Scott would probably be at second and so I wouldn't be.

Towards the beginning of July our team hosted a double-header against the team from Hammond; Scott's team. I don't remember the scores but I do recall between games that some of the parents bought pizzas for the boys on both teams. There were at least a handful of St. Paul's kids that were on either one of the teams. Scott and I were the only two from the opposing sides to sit and eat together. After we finished I remember him telling me that he would see me in the fall. Unfortunately, those were the last words that I heard from my friend.

Two weeks after the game my friend Nathan Murray and I were playing at the house. Nathan was a frequent at my place because we shared the same passion for baseball. I had asked my mom and dad if Nathan could spend the night but they said it was not such a good idea. After he left Dad sat me down and told me that Scott was the passenger in a car accident as he and his brother were traveling back to Hammond from working out at St. Paul's that morning. Scott died on impact. That kind of news is never easy to take at any age. At a fragile fourteen years old, I did not know how to handle it. I didn't handle it well. I kept it all in.

Scott Dottolo

III
And met some more along the way

Dad took me to Hammond for the visitation. It was one of the largest crowds I had ever seen. I had seen a few of my classmates as I was standing in line. They were much closer to Scott than I had been and to this day I have not spoken to them about how his death had impacted me. It didn't seem right. Really, there was not a person that I could actually talk to about this. My friends in Bogalusa had no idea who Scott was so they couldn't grasp words to tell me beyond *"I'm sorry"*. My friends (the ones I frequently associated with) at school I couldn't say anything to. I was afraid that it would seem that I was clinging to a tragedy that was shared by our entire class as my own personal trauma. Even if this didn't cross my mind, I would not have had the right words to say. Instead I chose to not say anything at all. I had reverted back to the 'me' that I hated to be.

My freshman year as a high school student was not all that bad. It was, though, as a student as St. Paul's. I didn't like it there at all. I did not feel like I belonged at the school. On the night of the homecoming dance, I stayed in my bed and pretended to be sick. I didn't have a date so I made up a reason why I couldn't attend. My presence did not seem to matter anyway. Based on the yearbook from my freshman year, this was the literal truth. I, Ryan Adams, was left out of the yearbook.

It was not an instance where the name was right and the picture was someone else. No. Mistakes are understandable but neither my name nor my picture was in the annual. This reality is embarrassing to admit but it is a rather accurate description of how I thought of myself as a St. Paul student. Ironically the only proof that I attended St. Paul's in 1995-96, was a baseball team picture in the sports section. Baseball was the one thing that kept me there. It was my constant. All was not lost though. The one way to forget about the tragedy that had happened the summer before was to just go another way. I did just that. I looked back home.

During the fall semester I had rekindled some friendships with a group that attended Bogalusa High School. My three best friends also happened to play (though not surprising) baseball for Bogalusa High. I did not have to jump through any hoops to be accepted in my hometown. I was accepted by association and it was easier to be myself.

I think what made me appreciate my buddies in Bogalusa so much was the simple fact that they got me out of the batting cage during the weekends. It took convincing but they stood beside me as I made the awkward transition into a social life. Every time they would ask me to go hang out with them, I would conjure up some lame excuse as to why I couldn't. Lucky for me they were persistent. I was appreciative.

The three friends: Timmy Pittman, Adam Cooper, and Jeff Tourne and I were always together on the weekends which meant that the weekdays were just that much longer. During that fall we all played in a fall baseball league in Covington. Because of the importance of baseball in South Louisiana, there were plenty of players in the league. The highlight of the fall league was playing in the Thanksgiving tournament in Baton Rouge. I think that is where my friendship with those guys seemed to escalate. Our team, since naturally my dad was one of the coaches, was composed of my three buddies from Bogalusa, a few guys that played at Covington High, and the rest were teammates of mine from St. Paul's. The experience was as complete as could be expected. I was playing baseball with all the guys I felt comfortable around. We were staying in the same hotel as a Teen Louisiana pageant and we got to walk through the lobby as if we were some elite team. We got to "act as if". I got to "act as if". It was surreal. Once it was over it was back to reality and back to school.

That spring, tryouts came around again. Because of the size of the junior and senior baseball classes at St. Paul's (and for the entire program for that matter), there were only a few spots available to play "up". By that I mean that few sophomores played on the varsity during the 1996 season. Therefore few freshmen played on the Junior Varsity team. There were enough prospective players to field a complete freshmen team. I was one of the lucky few who were asked to play with the Junior Varsity that season. I was proud to say the least. Besides, the Varsity had just purchased new sleeveless pinstriped uniforms that season which meant the old uniforms were going to be passed down for the JV. I got to wear the same uniform that had been worn in the state playoffs just the year before. It was a bright spot.

Throughout the spring semester of my freshman year my relationship with the Bogalusa boys continued. They would come over to the house almost nightly since they were playing Varsity as 9th graders and they wanted to get some extra swings in. I loved hitting with them and hanging out with them. Intrinsically, I wanted to showcase what I could do in comparison to my friends (Jeff, Timmy, Adam, Brett Baughman, and others) that were playing high school baseball. That motivation never ceased especially since I had to watch my buddies play St. Paul's during the two rounds of district play in games under the lights after the field was cleaned of the JV participants. In true to form, after each Bogalusa loss and St. Paul's victory, the boys and I would find something to do. It didn't matter to them the score of the game or whether or not we played against each other. I didn't have to prove anything to them. They appreciated me for who I was. I probably would have been better off if I had the same outlook about Ryan Adams that they did. But my perspective was different. My situation at St. Paul's made me have to look at things in another way. They weren't walking in my shoes.

Untitled (the 1ˢᵗ poem I ever wrote)

Over every mountain
Around every corner
There is always a new horizon
A new challenge, a minor set-back
Toward our everyday goal
Images of failure seek upon those who turn back
Yet those who strive for excellence find solutions to such images
And it is determination that sets us on this everlasting journey
To a new challenge
A new image
A new horizon

July 1998

IV
Had my share of slumps and errors

Sophomore year for any teenager is a pivotal time in a high school career. By the end of your first semester you are at the transition from the 8th grader entering into high school and the graduating senior that is off to face the college world. 1997, my sophomore year, was my movement towards the Ryan Adams I would be at graduation. It was no secret that I was generally unhappy at my school. My parents and I would have conversations (and sometimes arguments) about my contentment at St. Paul's. There was no way I would be going to Bogalusa but my parents were concerned about my happiness. The only thing that seemed to keep me at SPS was a sport that I had no guaranteed future in. I stayed at St. Paul's for baseball. I needed a reason, though, for it to be worth it. For the upcoming season, I would.

In January of 1997 I was given the opportunity to try-out for the St. Paul's varsity. Four underclassmen were asked; three sophomores and one freshman. With a team that had twelve seniors on the team; talent was abundant. Five of the seniors that year went on to play baseball at the next level. Needless to say, there was little margin for error. A senior second basemen and catcher had graduated the year before, so those spots were open for the season. Three of us who were trying out were all second basemen; the other was a catcher. The other two, Chuck Hickman (future Louisiana player of the year in 1999) and Andrew Mauldin (Coach Mauldin's youngest son), could pitch. I could not. Both Andrew and Chuck were much stronger than I was. The writing was on the wall as to how this was going to play out. The preseason conditioning was very difficult for me. I was, without a doubt, the weakest guy on the team. I quickly realized that I was not as prepared as I should have been. However, by the end of the tryout period it had become official. I had made the St. Paul's varsity baseball team. One of my goals had been achieved.

I remember going back to Bogalusa so excited. I knew I was going to play Junior Varsity in the season but that seemed to be beside the point. I was going to be on the team that was expected to be a contender for the State Championship. I was going to get my pinstriped uniform. I was going to get an official jersey number of my own. The jersey number was important. Athletes have an attachment to a number. I always wore the number 23 after my favorite ball player growing up, Ryne Sandberg. Unfortunately for me, the jerseys were determined by the size of the individual. I was stuck with number 8. I'll admit that it took a minute to grow on me but I soon came around. Ironically enough, the St. Paul's baseball field sat about a block away from 8th avenue and the road that stretched just beyond left field was Adams Street. I thought it was fitting that I could say that I literally played down from the corner of "Adams and 8th". Or at least that was how my mind worked. Needless to say, though, I was happy to just get a number No longer would I be "*hey you…what's your name again*", I would be "*hey number 8…what's your name again*".

One of the first people that I had decided to inform of my triumph was Mr. Terry Wood. Mr. Terry was my first little league coach. He was the only man to coach me before my dad. It seemed that Mr. Terry had been everyone's little league coach at one point in time. He was a heck of a nice guy and one of the few people that I knew of that had no problems telling you that he loved you. I remember that we were at a Mardi Gras function of some kind when I went and told him. He gave me his customary hug beforehand and afterwards said, *"Walter Ryan [everyone who knew me as a kid called me by my full name], I always knew you could do it...you were always talented but you didn't give yourself enough credit...I'm proud of you...and I love you"*. Coming from someone I admired like Mr. Terry that meant a lot. He now had said something that only a few others ever told me...that I had talent. Now, making the team at St. Paul's actually did feel like an accomplishment. I felt like I had fans in Bogalusa, rooting for me to do well. That was nice. This, of course, made it more difficult to want to leave. I didn't want to disappoint.

With the support that I had from back home, just making the team was not going to be enough for me. I was motivated but intimidated. Playing for Rick Mauldin can be intimidating. He is that type of coach. He was well-known for demanding the best out of his players. His came from a military family and was well traveled. He had been the head coach at St. Paul's for almost twenty years at this point. As an assistant at Jesuit High School in New Orleans he had been apart of a state championship team. That goal had yet to be obtained at St. Paul's. Coach Mauldin built the SPS baseball program from the ground-up and this team was poised to win the first state title in school history. With so much riding on the season, he expected every team member to be of state championship quality. Besides, a team is only as strong as its weakest player. On the 1997 St. Paul's baseball team, I was the weakest player. Yet, I knew that somewhere along the line I had made an impression on this man.

Besides being the head baseball coach, Rick Mauldin was also the disciplinarian at St. Paul's. My first encounter with him occurred after he had made an announcement about the fall baseball league. I nervously walked to his office and mumbled through introducing myself while asking for the fall league information. He did his homework on me. He knew I wasn't a trouble-maker. I fit the character of a St. Paul's baseball player. It was my talent that was in question. I know that he wanted me to do well. He wanted to find a place for the good kid. With my lack-of-physical strength and blatant nervousness, I made it pretty difficult to put me in. In fact, I only made one varsity appearance that season...as a pinch runner. Whether Coach Mauldin liked you or not, a lack of focus is unacceptable. That appearance would also be my last that season.

When all you have to do is get the sign, watch the bunt hit the ground, and run to second base, increased playing time should develop. Well, it should...unless (of course) you fail to watch the batter get the bunt down, almost get picked off between first and second base, somehow make it to second, then repeat the mistake again from second base but this time get out. What made matters worse was looking at all the faces of the players that were more-or-less perturbed by my running exploits. It was customary for Coach Mauldin to allow every member of the team to contribute in some way. I had blown my opportunity to contribute. Playing Ryan Adams in a varsity baseball game would be a liability. I became a quiet observer.

The best news from this experience was my move of positions from second to third. This, of course, I had been hinted at back during my 8th grade season. I played the position on the Junior Varsity. In my first game I made a diving play on a groundball and successfully threw the runner out at first base. I liked my new home. I was going to be groomed to be the next third baseman for St. Paul's baseball. Meanwhile, I was still a bench player for the varsity.

Being a bench player was never fun. But I was a bench player on one of the best teams in the state of Louisiana. We were a feared team throughout much of 1997. It was one of (if not the) most talented teams in St. Paul's history. The seniors were confident it was going to be their year. I was confident too. The practice shirt for the year was simple and direct "NOW OR NEVER". This was going to be the year that we would win it all. And if they (we) did, I was going to get a big state championship ring as well. In the first round we had two guys go 5 for 5 in the game. We had a dramatic finish in the quarterfinals and we were one win away from going to the state championship for the first time. I remember before the semi-final game against Parkway High School near Shreveport, Coach Mauldin approached me while our opponents were taking infield and just make some small talk. I remember saying with confidence that we would be back to this level again next year. I think I was just living in the moment. He nodded in agreement. I think we both understood that these seniors were St. Paul's best shot. It was a shot that we missed. We lost in the latter innings of the game and you could sense the disappointment among everyone. Some felt this would be nearing the end of St. Paul's baseball being among the elite programs. I guess it was appropriate that I arrive at the brink of our downfall.

A few decisions were made at the end of that sophomore season. The first, I was determined to no longer be the weakest on the team. I wanted to contribute. The second, I was tired of being an outsider. With a team that had twelve seniors on it, talent was abundant. if I wanted to be embraced at my school, then I would have to make a change. I would spend more time in Covington and spend more time around my teammates. Besides, we were the varsity now and almost by default. It seemed that after we lost in the semi-finals, all of the juniors on the team (with the exception of Coach Mauldin's oldest son Mathew) decided to quit. They thought we were going to be awful. That summer, they were right. We had only won one ballgame the entire summer. It was reminiscent of "all-star" days from little league. My play was also reminiscent of those 'all-star' days. I injured my arm throwing across the diamond at third base. Coach had decided to move back to second before the end but now I developed a fear of throwing short distances. A new dedication was needed. It didn't appear that I was going to be useful on the infield for next year's team.

My two decisions were also going to naturally have other consequences. The more time I spent trying to fit in the Covington-Mandeville area, the less time I spent in Bogalusa. It was impossible to be in two places at once. There was no way I could maintain that balance. I was growing tired of trying to maintain that balance. My decision went where it always seemed to go…the way of baseball.

To the best of my ability, I worked out on my own for the duration of the summer. If I was not going to be the best athlete, I wanted to be the most dedicated to my craft. I always had in my head that somewhere out there was a kid that was doing more than me to get better. That kid was who I was competing against on a daily basis. Dad understood this better than most. Both mom and dad were happy to see me opening up more with people outside of Bogalusa. It was not that they had anything against my friends from home but they also saw me on those lonely nights not one or two years before. They developed an idea that would benefit all three of us. They invested in an apartment that was close to the St. Paul's campus. Since mom worked at St. Tammany hospital merely two blocks away and I playing baseball around the corner, it seemed to make sense that we save gas money by not having three cars travel back and forth everyday. We were entering into a new start and enter I did as an upperclassmen at St. Paul's. It would be the year that changed my life forever.

V
But never told it to be this tough

Throughout the first few months of my junior year I was having a great time. My best friend, Morgan Strain, was now pretty much living with my parents and me in the apartment to save himself a trip from Slidell. Morgan and I had been friends since our freshmen year at St. Paul's. His aunt and my mother were close friends in high school, so we had a common background from the start. Morgan became one of the constants throughout my high school career. The great thing about our friendship is that it seemed that we were polar opposites of each other. I was the brains, he was not. He was popular and easy to get to know, I was not. We were good for each other.

Morgan was bound and determined to break me from my shell throughout our junior year. I was hesitant at first but I attended a few parties with him. He understood the concept of "guilty by association". However, in this case, it would be "accepted by association". His attitude was contagious for me and I was appreciative. I was slowly moving towards making a clean break from Bogalusa. I signed up to attend a trip to Washington D.C. for November. I attempted (though unsuccessfully) to run for a position on the student council. I was inching towards a new me. I still maintained my friendships in Bogalusa but things were different now. Jeff, probably my closest friend back home, had graduated from high school and was starting anew. Timmy was now involved in a serious relationship and Adam and I were just not the same without them. Morgan was opening up new doors and I liked the fact that my closest friend that I had had nothing to do with baseball. Then, things started to take a turn.

In October of my junior year, my grandmother (Beezie) passed away. Like any loss, it took something out of me. I remember a few weeks afterwards, I had gone down to Bogalusa to go out for the weekend. Bogalusa High School was having a Halloween dance. Dances were often fun nights. In Bogalusa, though, they were usually a hit-or-miss type deals. Some were better than others. Anyway, I was in the parking lot of Delchamps grocery store and one of my old childhood friends Brett Baughman came up to me.

Brett and I grew up together. We attended each others' birthday parties. We were both taught by my mom and went through Annunciation together until I left for St. Paul's. We played little league together. In fact, in those sixth and seventh grade all-star summers Brett had been the one that got the winning hit in our lone victory. He was also notorious for losing his temper when he played. Brett had assumed the nickname of "mad dog". In out last all-star outing (one in which we lost by a mere 24 runs), Brett was having a rather off day. At one point of the game he was playing in center field and somehow a fly ball found a way to hit him in the chest. Instead of staying on the ground or leaving the game due to injury, Brett just tensed up like (well) a mad dog. Baseball was important to Brett but it didn't burden his life in the way that it did mine.

Brett was one of the guys I had to watch playing for Bogalusa High School. We were, by no means, the best of friends but when you are around people since diapers, you grow a special bond. Brett and I did not usually hang with the same crowds. He listened to rap music. He had a speaker system in his Intrepid. He wore more baggy clothes. I, on the other hand, listened to rock, still had factory speakers in my Honda, and was more-or-less on the preppy side of life. But one thing about Brett and I is that we always talked to each other whenever we came in contact. We never lost sight of the past we shared. He came up to me that night in the parking lot and told me that he had heard about my grandmother and wanted to tell me he was sorry. Our conversation only lasted a few minutes but we both mentioned that we were looking forward to finally playing against each other in the upcoming year. We would never get that chance. Two weeks after this conversation, I got the phone call.

Adam Cooper called me at around 9 o'clock at night and told me that Brett and another childhood friend Krissy had been in an accident. I asked him if they were okay and he said that he thought they were. To be honest, I left it at that and thought I would just go and check on him the next day after school. When I arrived at the apartment, mom (unusually) was already home. She mentioned that I go get changed and so we could go to the hospital in New Orleans. I asked if everything was okay with Brett. Her short answers gave me an indication. On the way to the hospital I kept replaying the conversation I had with Brett just a few weeks earlier. I couldn't wrap my head around how I just assumed from Adam's tone when he called that everything was going to be okay. But everything was going to be alright. Maybe the accident was more serious than I thought but I wasn't going to lose my childhood buddy. When we arrived I learned something about hospital visitation protocol that I hadn't known before. When visiting hours are over and they are still allowing people to stay, it means that you are not there to visit. It means that you are there to say good-bye.

It was about ten-thirty at night when I was able to go back. The young man that I saw was not the friend I knew growing up. I didn't recognize him. In the hallway I had mentally prepared myself for what I was going to say. I wasn't prepared for this. Tears immediately swelled once I caught my first glimpse of Brett. Any word of encouragement I might have had was taken away. It is hard to describe but my mind was simultaneously racing and blank. Instinctively, I turned to his mother, Mrs. Kaye, and the only words I could muster as I gave her a hug was *"I'm sorry"*. By the next day, my childhood friend was gone.

The next days at school I could not maintain my focus. The teachers had been made aware that the Bogalusa boys had lost a dear friend of theirs. A few of them came up to me and tried to console me. It was no hope. I didn't want to talk to *them*. The entire day I wanted to just not be at school. Rather, I didn't want to be at this school. I wanted to talk to people from Bogalusa. The feelings were similar to how it was for Scott, except this time it was in reverse. I felt that I had abandoned my life in Bogalusa and this was my form of punishment. I had to watch all these students move on about their day as if nothing in the world was wrong. It seemed cruel that the world around me did not stop to wonder why I looked so sad. The truth was that I did want someone to notice and not because they had been forewarned. I wanted desperately for anybody to walk up to me and just tell that my mannerisms were not as they should have been. Then again, the truth was I also wanted them to keep their distance. How do you bring up the conversation to other people without breaking down? How could I have possibly let them know what was going on in my head? I didn't know what was going on in my head. It was not their faults that they didn't know. But I didn't care. Logic left me at 10:30 the night before. I had to have something to blame this on.

By the end of the week I was back in Bogalusa amongst my friends. The entire weekend was surreal. Everything was happening so fast. There was no manual as to the best way to handle the death of a teenager. So everyone grieved in their own manner. What was important to us is that we at least were in it together. Mrs. Kaye had asked me to be one of the pall-bearers for Brett's funeral. The other guys that she asked were all of us that had grown up with Brett and not necessarily all the guys he hung out with at high school. I accepted the offer. I mentioned to her that it was an honor that she thought of me in this regard. We, the pall-bearers, were the last to see Brett prior to the closing of the casket and had the haunting task of carrying our friend through a sea of faces towards his grave-site. It would be among the longest walks I would ever have to make.

On the day of the funeral, Mrs. Kaye had asked three people to speak the eulogies for Brett. All of them shared in one connection to Brett. They all had been his baseball coach. My father and Coach Mack went together as they had been our coaches for the majority of our years playing little league. Dad read aloud words that my mom had written the night before. It had been a job well done. I was proud of the poise that my father had shown under the circumstances. But it was the third man that spoke that Saturday morning that captured the room. Mr. Terry Wood (the man I considered a mentor) really got to everyone's emotions. Besides, it was Mr. Terry (as I mentioned before) that had seemingly coached everyone in that room at one point or another. We all could relate to him. We all had received the familiar hugs and reminders from this man as to how much he loved us. As he had done for me when I made the St. Paul's varsity roster, he never seemed to miss an opportunity to let us know.

I recall that as Mr. Terry stood in front of the crowd he mentioned of the first time Brett came to practice and his equipment did not fit. *"But now"*, he said, *"He is playing on God's team. His equipment will always fit and he never has to worry again"*. He then talked directly to Brett's little brother Jeffrey. He wished that Jeffrey could have known the man his brother would become. By this point, I lost it. We all wish we could have known the man Brett would become. My heart went out to Mrs. Kaye, Mr. Ricky, and Jeffrey. The reality of what was taking place kept hitting me repeatedly in the chest.

After the service the pall-bearers rode in my vehicle toward the cemetery. Brett's gravesite was located only a short distance from my grandparents; in the back corner of the cemetery. It was now time to gather the strength to carry his casket towards the location I would come to visit on numerous future occasions. The image of that walk has never escaped my mind. Somehow the burial did not seem to be a proper good-bye. I didn't find consolation that my buddy was in a better place. How was I supposed to move on from here? How was I supposed to maintain my composure tomorrow or the next day? I had been comforted the past few days by the presence of my other friends. Talking to them did not allow me time to think. With the service now over, I would have too much time. In my state of mind, that wasn't necessarily a good thing.

Brett and I in Tuxedos July 1997

VI
...And you're asked to sacrifice

After the funeral, I played a baseball game the very next day. It seemed cruel to have to play. It seemed worse that none of my teammates really knew how my Saturday had gone. Some say the best way to overcome heartache is to find a sense of normalcy. I normally spent my fall weekends on a baseball diamond. The game was forgettable in the sense that I can not recall the score of the game nor whom we played. I remember not being physically able to do anything right. Maybe it was good enough for me to just be there. Maybe just showing up that day meant that, subconsciously, I was putting myself in a position to move forward. I didn't think so.

In the following weeks, my parents started to worry about me. Tough to admit now but they should have been. There was a distinct change in my behavior. I wasn't acting out or getting into trouble at school. It was nothing of that nature but I was acting not myself. After four years at St. Paul's, I was finally starting to enjoy it and I was coming out-of-my-shell when all this happened. This death, I couldn't let go. I stopped my attempt at normalcy in Covington and reverted back the Ryan Adams, the introvert. Nothing made sense. I was ashamed, confused, scared, angry, and mournful at the same time. I kept asking questions to God and felt that I received no answers. Even though I knew others shared in my pain, it seemed that this was all coming down on me. Why me? Why now? Why was I being punished? I thought that I was a good kid. What had I done to deserve this pain? Could I get a sign that everything is going to be okay? Could I get some kind of indication that I was going to be alright? At those moments I would await an answer to these questions. My faith had been tested. I was certain that no answers would come. For the time being I did what I thought was best. I stopped caring.

The people I wanted to talk to each day, I didn't see on a daily basis. Morgan tried to help but it was to no avail. He probably understood my situation better than anyone but I knew that he didn't have the words. No one had the words. Mom and Dad were caught between trying to give me the appropriate space and intervening to ensure that I didn't stray too far off the beaten path. Like I mentioned, they should have been worried about me. Though I had never been clinically diagnosed, it was safe to deduce that at the age of 16, I was battling depression. Adversity had never been my strong-suit. As I had done after Scott, I relied on my only outlet, crutch that I had…baseball.

Baseball, now, made me angry. Each time I didn't hit the ball right or I made an error or I saw others getting stronger than myself, I got irate. I wrongfully took my frustrations out on my father. He still went into the batting cage with me as he had always done. He just wanted his son to get better. I knew that it hurt him; watching his youngest seemingly self-destruct in front of his eyes. I was very cognitive that my approach to things was not the best route to be taken. I knew that my anger was not going to fill my void. At the time, though, rationale took a back seat to emotion.

Though baseball had been the routine outlet, I attempted other means to ease my pain. I was aware that my approach had been an unhealthy measure. Maybe if I could help others, I could relieve some of my own sorrows. The first thing that I wanted to do was to develop something for Brett. After Scott had passed away his father, Mr. Sonny, had little football patches made in his honor. On them were Scott's number (#5) and the phrase "lil bud power". There were a number of people who had one. I had mine on the back of my letterman jacket. In an attempt to do the same for Brett, I asked dad to help me get patches made for Brett. I designed them in the shape of a baseball, in Bogalusa colors (black and gold), and on them I put Brett's name and the phrase "friends are friends forever". The song "friends are friends forever" had been played at Brett's funeral. I thought it to be appropriate. My thoughts were to give patches to the entire Bogalusa baseball team and his friends at the high school. Of course, I kept a few for myself and some for Brett that I could keep updated at his gravesite.

Within weeks after the deaths of Brett and my grandmother, I did something almost on whim. I began to write. I might as well have. I wasn't talking to anyone else. I began my journal. At first, it was meant to be kept private but that measure didn't last long. If I ever got an entry that I felt to be potent, I would share it with a few of my friends who were willing to listen. Morgan frequently enjoyed listening to what I wrote. It was among his more admirable qualities. I think he knew that just being an ear for my thoughts was going to be apart of the healing process. In a way, his willingness to be my frequent audience kept the pen to the pad. It gave me something to look forward to. Writing certainly became a safe outlet for me.

In a way (though tough to admit), I wrote some entries as if they were going to be the last words written by Ryan Adams. There were some entries that I didn't wish for Morgan to see just yet. I didn't want anyone not to know what was going on in my mind. But I also didn't want to relinquish all this information to my best friend. I frequently imagined that if my funeral was to come, that I would have the appropriate words to say. I wouldn't leave it to someone else. In comparison to the other thoughts that ran through my head, these were probably the safest. I didn't want to reflect on paper the helplessness that I had battled. Helpless is not how I desired to appear going into the baseball season I had been preparing for since I walked onto campus.

As had happened every year, January came around and a new season at St. Paul's baseball was about to begin. The season that I had anticipated ever since I made the decision to go to St. Paul's in the 8th grade, ever since I watched my buddies play while I watched from the other side of the fence, ever since I had the taste of being a game away from a state championship. That season was here, but had lost some of its luster. This time, expectations were not as high as they had been in the past. Not for me and not for the team.

Based on our performance the summer before, we were predicted to finish fourth in our district; even behind Bogalusa. I guess it was understandable: one senior, only three guys with experience (I wouldn't count my one recorded out as experience), and two freshmen starting. The predictions were pretty safe. We had not given reason for anyone to have faith in us. Some had mentioned to Coach Mauldin that there would be no way this team could be successful. Others mentioned this to a rebuilding year. Honestly, how feasible would it be for us to (all of a sudden) replace the most talented team in school history? I had originally thought the summer before that I would step up as one of the leaders of the team. I had wanted to achieve the impossible. The event of the fall

I had put a damper on those plans; also I had not proven myself to be capable of such a position. To add to matters, my role on the team had changed right after we started. I was being moved from the infield to the outfield.

I knew it was for the best. I was a realist and understood that I was being moved because I wasn't playing well enough to stay on the infield. I had already been moved from my customary position at second base to third. I was now moving from third to left field. When Coach Mauldin pulled me aside to notify me of the changes, he had thought that my feelings were hurt. Because I had grown accustom to hiding my emotions at school, the truth behind my eyes was that of relief. I was only disappointed in the fact that I thought that I let people down. Irregardless, playing in the outfield required less thinking. My thoughts had been a detriment to my level of play even before I arrived at St. Paul's. Since Brett's passing, my thoughts had been a detriment off the field as well. Coach Mauldin may not have realized when he did it but allowing me to think less was the best thing for such a fragile player. And I would get even more fragile. I was about to be broken.

Scott Patch

Brett Patch

VII
...Each day I prepare myself

As a junior, I was apart of the Mardi Gras court in Bogalusa. At the party that night Mr. Terry came up to our table and said to me, *"Walter Ryan...you know that I coached all of you boys at this table...* yes sir, you sure did...*well you know what Walter Ryan...*what's that Mr. Terry...*and I love every single one of you"*. Those were the last words that Mr. Terry ever shared with me. Five days later, he was gone. I thought that after Brett had died I thought I had hit rock-bottom. I was wrong. I was scared as to how far this was going to go. I grew numb.

It seemed that each time I was even remotely close to anything resembling recovery, someone else died. For a kid that wanted desperately to break out, it seemed I spent more time in funeral homes and at gravesites than I did hanging out with my friends. For a player who at first just wanted to prove that he belonged and then prove that he had talent, it appeared that I had more patches on the back of my lettermen jacket of dead friends than I did patches on my arm of personal achievements. Besides that, the drive between Bogalusa and Covington left more time for my mind to roam.

Thirty-five minutes is a long way between two cities. When you make that drive as frequently as I had, Highway 21 became the definition of a lonely road. I would be lying if I told you I didn't consider veering off. If there was any consolation in the recent event then it was from the letter read aloud at Mr. Terry's funeral. Mrs. Kaye had written, *"If Brett is playing on God's team, he was awaiting for someone to coach"*. That was my only consolation and it wasn't much. It didn't take any of the pain away. I had been asking for God to provide me with an answer that everything was going to be alright. Instead, one of the men I looked up in this world was taken away. I had moved to a point that was past hurt.

My approach to baseball was changing following the death of Mr. Terry. I didn't care anymore. I didn't get nervous anymore. Why should I? I faced the hard reality of losing multiple loved ones; what pitcher was going to scare me? I helped carry my friend's casket through a sea of crying teenagers, what fly ball was too tough to get to? I was nervous about who was going to die next, how was a game supposed to make me nervous? The answer was simple. It didn't. And for the first time in my life…I stood out.

There was one Saturday practice that I got my first glimpse of what was to come that season. Morgan would sometimes arrive to watch our practices and on this particular Saturday he drove his truck up to left-center field while we were taking fly-balls. Customary to our practice routine, someone else was hitting live batting practice while the flies were being hit. If you could get a good read on the ball you were to make an effort. From over the fence Morgan yelled, *"Hey Ryan…I came to see you do something…now impress me"*. By that time, a deep fly ball was hit to my left. I ran and laid-out just to see if I could get close. Morgue nearly jumped over the fence with excitement. It was a taste. I was showing people that I was good enough. People were beginning to recognize who number 8 was playing out in left field and, damn, it felt good.

Our team in 1998 began the season playing as it had throughout the previous summer and we lost our first game by ten runs. We lost the second game as well and then we sort of just stopped losing. In an effort to change up the batting order, Coach Mauldin surprised us all when he announce that I was batting second (I had not batted higher than sixth any other year). I guess Coach Mauldin felt the "two-hole" would be a good spot to try. I wasn't a homerun threat *(remember I had never hit one...ever)* but I did a fair enough job of getting on base. As it worked out, I would remain at that spot the rest of the season. With the lack of multiple seniors, I began to justify myself in a leadership role. I felt that our season was starting to become a reflection of me. I was finally allowing my actions say what my mouth never had the guts to. I had confidence that I had not had before. I was playing with reckless abandonment. We were playing like a team possessed. With fortunes 'seemingly' starting to change, with a new found perspective, and with a new state of mind, I decided to make what was, for me, a drastic course of action.

Our religion teacher, Joe Kight *(for whom I owe a debt of gratitude)*, had given the class an assignment in which we were to give a speech about a person that reflected the idea of "Christian Moral Man". Mr. Kight was in his first year at the school and he had developed an attachment to me and my situations. He had made it a point to try to help me overcome my pain. I don't believe even he thought that I was going to use this assignment as a vessel. We were to research the person's background and make sure that they fit the criteria for the assignments rubric. I never quite did the assignment as it was asked however I was one of the first to volunteer to speak. When we received our instructions I knew right away that

I was going to talk about Mr. Terry. They say that public speaking is among people's biggest fears. Before that day, I would have agreed. I stood in front of a class of thirty young men (the same ones that I did not want to develop an opinion of me) and I just talked about Mr. Terry and about the eulogy he gave at Brett's funeral. By the time I got to the funeral part, the tears were already pouring down and then when I told them that only a month an a half ago he had also died, my emotions were uncontrollable. As I completed the speech I told the members of the class, that if they thought less of me for crying in front of them that day…I did not care. If they don't respect me…I did not care. And to Mr. Kight (who had tears as well), if this is not what you were looking for in this assignment…I did not care. I did what I did because it was what I felt I needed to do. Then I sat down and when class ended, I walked out.

Over the next few days, a small contingent of my classmates mentioned to me that it took a lot of nerve to say what I did. They told me that they were proud of me and they were sorry because they just didn't know. Their sentiments were appreciated and finally I had come to terms with one of the deaths. I said what I wanted to about Mr. Terry Wood. For once, I utilized an opportunity.

The speech that I gave occurred in the first week of March. We were still early into our baseball season but I and the team were, again, playing well. We were building momentum going into the opening round of district play. Our first game had been circled on my calendar since the schedule had been released. I no longer believe in coincidence or in chance. I believe now, as I was beginning to then. There was something definitive about that opening date. On March 17th 1998, we would play the first district game at home… against Bogalusa.

VIII
To Be the King of Diamonds

On the day of the Bogalusa game, it was hard to contain my excitement. By the way were playing and the history between the two teams, the result of a St. Paul's victory was expected. I wasn't anxious as to how the game would turn out. This was my day. There had been so much built up in my mind leading to this game. From the moment I woke up that morning I began counting down the hours until the first pitch. When I walked to campus from the apartment, a visit to Coach Mauldin's office was on my agenda. There was a question (favor rather) that I needed to ask him in person.

During the school day I found my way to see Coach with my request. He had known all that was going on with me, but it was not something that we ever talked about. Besides the speech in religion class, I had grown accustomed to not mentioning the ones I had lost in the recent months. My lone request that day was to see if I could wear Brett's patch on my uniform. I had given the patches to the Bogalusa team to wear on their uniforms but had yet to wear one for myself. I had wanted this night to be my first.

I didn't know how Coach Mauldin would react to this request. He had made it a point that we not try to make ourselves individuals on the baseball field. If one person wore their socks high, then we all wore our socks high. We had a dress code for practice attire. That was just St. Paul's baseball. With that being said, Coach Mauldin did not mind at all that I wear the patch. This was an occasion that an exception could be made. He understood what this game meant to me. He knew tonight was a little more than a 7 inning affair between district opponents.

After school had gotten out I rushed home to change and went straight over to the baseball field. I would customarily take a little time to settle my thoughts and get focused on what I had to do that night. There was no time for focus. The Bogalusa bus had already arrived as both the JV and Varsity traveled together for the game. My friends from the Bogalusa team were all relaxing on the visiting bleachers when I walked up. We spent most of the time just making small talk until my buddy Timmy Pittman asked me what I would do if he hit a home run over my head in left field that night. As every group of friends has the one big guy that nobody messes with… Timmy was ours. He was one of those 'corn-fed' white boys that just knew how to be athletic. At 6'3", 240lbs we expected Timmy to hit tape-measure shots when he got the opportunity (of course, as long as he played St. Paul's he would get a heavy dose of off-speed pitches). The same was not expected of me. I told Timmy that if he hit one tonight that I would tip my cap to him as he rounded the bases. I then asked him what he would do if I hit one. Tim joked, *"if you hit one…I'll tell you what…after your boys get done with you at home plate…I'll give you a hug"*. We all continued our normal banter. The scenario we just talked about wasn't likely to happen… it never happened before.

There may have been one other game in my career to which I was as emotionally charged. It was not as much Bogalusa versus St. Paul's. It was Ryan playing in dedication to the people he lost. It was a relief to put behind all that had been built up for years of wanting to play and for months that I wanted to recover. What I failed to realize was that all of those moments that I had spent struggling in the batting cage trying to prove that I was worthy, every moment that I drove down that lonely highway, and for every minute I sat beside the graves doubting myself was about to come to fruition. I spent many hours following the deaths of Brett and Mr. Terry questioning the existence of God. I had routinely asked for some type of indication that everything was going to be alright; that I was going to be alright. I learned in one moment that God had a plan for Ryan Adams. The answer I had been seeking came in the form of a fastball in the third inning of the ballgame. With the count at 3 balls 1 strike, the pitcher, Donald Manuel, threw a fastball. I had a good swing at the pitch (probably one of my best swings) and I fouled that fastball straight back. I turned to Timmy (whom was catching) and said, *"Timmy, don't let Donald throw that again"*.

Before Donald was in his wind-up to deliver the 3-2 pitch, something was suddenly different. There was a sense of calm in my body. In an instant I knew that everything was going to be alright. I saw the pitch so clearly when I began my swing. I witnessed the ball leave the bat as it had never done so in any prior swing that I took. Instinctively, I put my head down to run to first base. I never saw exactly where the ball landed. I had never hit a home run before…until then.

I never saw the pitch ever go over the fence but by the time I reached first base I had seen the reaction of Coach Nunez (the 1st base coach) and I knew it was gone. If for a cowboy 8 seconds feels like a lifetime, then so did the 8 seconds it took me to round first base. The gravity of the situation overcame me. As lonely as I had felt for the past few months, I came to quickly realize as I continued my first homerun trot, the number of people that just knew. Equaling the joy of my first ever homerun was the fashion in which it was received. I didn't expect the homerun nor did expect what happened next.

As I rounded first base, to my surprise, was Adam Cooper (my friend that had called me about Brett) whom had stepped into the baseline from his position at second to shake my hand. *Was this really happening?* The rest of the infield did the same thing. I looked at the pitcher, Donald, and he tipped his cap. I could not clearly see Coach Mauldin as tears were swelling in my eyes but I know that I saw him smile. As I rounded 3rd base for the last 90 feet of my first home run, I did see all 6'3" of Timmy. He was standing behind my teammates (who had crowded at home plate) with a grin from ear to ear.

Within the next ten feet that I jogged, a new realization dawned on me. Over the next 8 seconds, I noticed that not only were the St. Paul fans standing and cheering but the Bogalusa fans were standing and cheering. With a smile on my face and tears in my eyes, I touched the plate and got mauled by my teammates. Timmy was a man of his word and gave me the hug we joked about hours before. Overcome with emotion, I touched the patch, took off my helmet, pointed to the sky.....and finally took a breath. For the moment, I had reached a pinnacle. I knew that I had a purpose. What just happened is what they write books about and have movies about. It doesn't really happen like that in real life. Except, it just did happen and it happened to me. Forever I would remember the night of March 17th, 1998. It was the night that God used a baseball to save me and provide a direction for my life. It was the night I, Walter Ryan Adams, was to be the king of diamonds.

His story's song

The lyrics of man throughout all of history
Have withstood the tests of time
From these, a human song debuts
This written one is mine
Twas a boy that started this march
Unknowing the way to go
Never did he consider all who watched over him
Or what inside him he bestowed
Never could he comprehend
Why his own lyrics he would write
Until he let down his guard and picked up a pen
Could he ascertain meaning to his life
Into frozen moments I watch this boy become a man
In his march along the path
Both he and I wonder about our future endeavors
And even more, their aftermath
For every man comes to doubt
In a trial he has met
Allowing such, though, to end the journey
Means denying glory that has not happened yet
He has come to face that on this voyage
Will come sorrow and also pain
Yet as a believer he, within him, feels
That one day forever embedded will be his name
No room is there for doubt
In the horizon that awaits
To understand is his motive
To inspire is his fate
Through the years he has marched
And march he will along
For the strides he makes will give music to
The lyrics of his story's song

July 2004

IX
Sometimes I can help coach someone

The day after I had my defining moment, I was treated no differently than I had been any other day at St. Paul's. No one really needed to treat me differently. I knew it wouldn't last. The footsteps I made would be erased in time, but there still would be few who knew they were mine. The game on March 17th was a blip on the sports page…a footnote in the standings. I visited Coach Mauldin in his office the next day at school. He said that his son Andrew told him after the game, "*I think there were some people upstairs that were looking over Ryan's homerun tonight*". To the vast majority, I had helped St. Paul's in a 13 run rout of Bogalusa high school. To a select few, the events from the previous night meant so much more. When I went back to Bogalusa the next day, I found out to whom.

As was customary each time I came back to town, I went to the cemetery first. For a while this became an unhealthy habit. The cemetery was located across the highway from my neighborhood. My grandparents, Brett, and Mr. Terry were all buried in close proximity to each other. This time, though, there was no grieving. I was going to deliver a message. There had been a bench placed near Brett's grave for the frequent visits he received over the past few months. The grass to the side of the grave had been worn from wear people often sat and only dirt remained. When I arrived at Brett's gravesite I saw a note written in the dirt. It was to Brett from Mrs. Kaye. It read simply, *"Ryan hit one for you last night…love Mom"*.

I had arrived that day to tell him myself. When I saw the note my eyes immediately began to swell. I would learn that Mrs. Kaye had received a phone call the night before to let her know about what had occurred. When she heard about the homerun she broke down. She had been asking for an answer to prayer as well. The single hit from the night before was Mrs. Kaye's indication just as it had been mine. Playing baseball had gained another meaning. I was helping a mother cope. I was helping myself cope. I was still unafraid but now I had regained some motivation as the season marched on.

Mrs. Kaye did not attend many of the Bogalusa games that season. It was too hard. She did make an exception for the St. Paul's game that was played at Bogalusa. I remember the game vividly because I only got one at bat. I had been sick the day before and was still recovering on the day of the Bogalusa game. When I tried to warm-up with the team, Coach Mauldin pulled me to the side and reminded me that I was in no condition to play. I was determined to play in that game. Coach made no promises but instead just told me to rest on the bench. He needed me to be healthy. The Bogalusa players had made it apart of their pre-game to gather at a sign in right field that had been dedicated to Brett to say a prayer. Since I wasn't able to warm up, the only running I had prior to the first pitch was meeting them in right field to join in the prayer.

There was no way I was going to start that game. There was little chance I was going to play. The appearance I did get took some coaxing. My lone at-bat came at the request of Mrs. Kaye whom had walked to Coach Mauldin and introduced herself to him between innings. She told him that she had come to see Ryan play and if it was possible, it would mean a lot for her to see me do just that. Along with not standing out as an individual, talking to spectators during a game was another 'no-no' of St. Paul's baseball. As it happened in the first game against Bogalusa, Coach made an exception to his rule. With a comfortable lead, Mrs. Kaye got her request and I was to pinch-hit for my lone at-bat of the afternoon. I wasted no time in my plate appearance and I swung at the first pitch that I saw. I was typically a pull hitter but in this at-bat the ball jumped off the bat and traveled towards right field. Brett's sign was in right-center field and the ball hit the sign. I got a stand-up double. I was in no condition to play. Then again, I don't think I was the one who was hitting that ball. It was the last time Mrs. Kaye ever saw me play. I wanted to make her proud.

X

In my own Cooperstown

With the conclusion of the Bogalusa series and the rest of district play, St. Paul's entered into the playoffs as district champs. The same team that was supposed to be one of the worst teams in St. Paul's history was steamrolling into the playoffs. Coach Mauldin had said that we were the biggest group of overachievers that he had ever seen. Considering my own abilities, he was accurate in this statement. It was great to know that I had a lot to do with that. Before the playoffs began Coach Mauldin sat us all in the dugout to inform who had made the all-district teams. Being an all-district player would have been an honor to have. At St. Paul's it was more than just having your name in the paper or gaining a patch for your letterman jacket. If you were all-district, that is how you were known to future SPS baseball players. If ever former players would return to campus Coach would introduce with their all-district title included. It was how you knew you belonged in the upper echelon of the program.

He sat us in the dugout prior to our first 'play-off' practice and told us he wanted to just let us know the results of the district meetings before we read about them in the papers. He said that despite being the district champs, some of us were going to be glad and some of us were going to be disappointed. Immediately, I thought I was going to be one of the ones to be disappointed. The all-district selection process requires the input of all the district coaches. They each bring in the team stats, compare players, and nominate players to 1st team, 2nd team, and so on. Each coach usually has a certain player(s) that he needs to maneuver in order to get other players the recognition. Knowing the process, I was unaware where I fit on the bargaining table. To my surprise, Coach Mauldin shared the good news first. *"One of our own was selected as the top rated outfielder in the entire district. Ryan, you were named 1st team all-district".* To be the top rated outfielder meant that the other coaches put me at the first position on the board. I was flattered. Moreover, I was now going to join the company of some of the better players in school history. I had gone from *"hey you"* to *"hey number 8"* to *"1st team all-district St. Paul's leftfielder #8 Ryan Adams"*. I had reached a new milestone. I could become one of the famed Rick Mauldin's stories. I was the kid not good enough to play the infield that moved to the outfield and gave an all-district (also all-parish) performance. My work was not done though. I wanted to help lead us to a championship and we had five opponents to go through to get there.

In the first round I went two for three with two doubles and we won in the bottom of the seventh inning against Pineville. Personally, this game was one of my defining moments as a player and one of my fondest memories. In the top of the seventh inning I was playing in left field with game tied. One of the 'perks' of playing left field at St. Paul's happened to be the unofficial placement of the student section. Two of my buddies were barbecuing on the other side of the fence and the aroma flowed onto the field of play. With the intensity of being in a time game (and the smell from behind me), I began to develop "cotton-mouth" and started to feel a little sick to my stomach. When the third out was recorded my focus shifted to just not throwing up. To make matters worse, I was due to lead off the bottom of the seventh. Ryan Spencer, our 3rd baseman, came to me with a routine comment that we always said to the person leading off the inning, *"You get on…I'll get you in".* *"Dude"*, I said, *"If I run I am pretty sure I'm going to puke".* *"I'm just going to try to hit one out".* Ryan looked a little unsure as to how to respond as I walked to the plate.

I knew that I didn't want the at-bat to last very long. If the first pitch was there, I was going to take a shot. As the first pitch was delivered, I wasted no time in starting my swing. The ball took off the bat towards left field but to my dismay it hit the fence in the air. Luckily, in my trip to second base, I had not gotten sick. In my mind, it was only a matter of time. Two quick outs were recorded and I was stranded on 2nd when Spencer came to bat. If there was any hit to the outfield, I was going to have to beat the throw to the plate. With two strikes, Ryan hit the ball to right field, and as soon as I turned the corner at 3rd I noticed everyone jumping in jubilation. Spencer had hit a home run and he had bailed me out from embarrassment on the grandest stage we had played to that point.

The rest of the playoffs had very similar luster to the first round. In the second round we scored seven runs with two outs to defeat Baker High School; won handedly in the quarterfinals before facing Parkway High School in the semi-finals. Parkway had been the same location in which we came up short for our state championship bid the year before. It was a bit of irony. As a sophomore bench player the year before, I told Coach Mauldin that we would be back here. At the time I had been talking figuratively but we, literally, were back in the exact same spot; one win away from the school's first state championship appearance.

As it turned out, Parkway was as stellar as advertised. All season long we had overcome our opponents having more talent than us. On this day, it was not to be the case. Parkway ended our season in five innings and would move on to play our district's runner-up in the state finals. The magical run had come up just short. We ended the season back where I promised Coach Mauldin we would be the year before. We were back to back semi-finalists. It was a remarkable feat. Our lone regret was that we could not win a championship for the only senior on the team, Mathew Mauldin. The rest of us would all be returning; knowing that we had proven ourselves to belong as one of the state's top teams. We had far exceeded expectations. The supposed worst team in St. Paul's history had equaled what only one other team at the school had done. We just knew what lied ahead. Why not us? Next year, we were going to be the first group to bring St. Paul's a baseball state championship.

XI
It's the approach that I bring to each at bat

My junior year of high school was by far the most memorable of my life. After the successful baseball season and a breakthrough for myself personally, I felt that I had overcome a great deal of obstacles. The success from the spring had given me a new lease on life. My outlook towards everything had been altered. Through the speech in religion class, I had made my peace with the death of Mr. Terry. With the home run, I felt that had come to peace with Brett. There was still something that I felt I needed to do. With my journal entries becoming something that I had come to enjoy, I decided to write a letter. The letter I was to write was addressed to someone whom I had never talked to before and had seen only once. I wrote to Mrs. Kathy Dottolo (Scott's mom).

It had been nearly four years since Scott had passed away in the summer after our 8th grade year. I wanted to finally let someone know what exactly his friendship meant in the short time that I knew him. While writing, I questioned as to whether I was doing the right thing. I didn't know how they had coped. Moreover, I was unsure as to how my letter would be received. So, needless to say, I was nervous. I was hesitant while writing and even more putting it in the mailbox. I had not told anyone (Morgan, my parents) what I was doing. This was personal. It was something that I wanted to do. Rather, it was something that I had to do. To this day, it is still among the proudest thing I have ever done.

I cannot recall all that I put in that letter but I remember vividly how it began. *Dear Mrs. Kathy...You may not ever remember hearing my name or recall ever seeing my face but my name is Ryan Adams and I wanted to tell you what your son meant to me.* Almost everything I have ever written, I have allowed someone to read beforehand. This was an exception. Within about two week's time, I received a letter back in the mail from Mrs. Kathy. Very similar to the message that Mrs. Kaye left besides Brett's grave, Mrs. Kathy said that my letter had been an answer to prayer. She mentioned that she was constantly discovering each day how far reaching the impact of her son went. Her response brought a tear and I was satisfied that I was able to make her smile. Besides, it was her son that taught me the meaning of what a few words can do.

After I got the note back from Mrs. Kathy, I let my mom read it and she was proud of what I had done. Mom always had a unique perspective of my experiences. We, of course, shared the natural relationship of mother and son, but Kathi Adams was also my first grade teacher. She knew me as a student. She knew my personality. She had seen the effects of asthma, baseball, school, and relationships had taken on her son. She was often not caught by surprise. This letter had. While I had made efforts to reach out to the mothers of my two friends, I had failed to recognize entirely the toll the incidents had taken on my own mom. She had also taught

Brett. She and Mrs. Kaye had been pregnant with us at the same time. Each time I had to go through the experiences I did, I'm sure she feared the distance created in the relationship between her and her baby boy. I had come to believe that everything happened for a reason. I knew my message to the Dottolo family had been well received. They now knew what I had wanted to say for four years. At the same time, it was a message to mom. She had an indication of how far I had come; that she had raised me right. Through all that had happened (especially in the last year) she had not lost me. I thought this to be the entirety to the letter I wrote that July. It was only the beginning. I (as we all do) needed to be reminded of my purpose. Over the course of my senior year, I would encounter the members of the Dottolo family; each of them approaching with a familiar message. The words exchanged (though few) were my indications that I needed to finish what I started. The first occurred at a football game that fall.

Coach Mauldin had asked me and another player to sell programs at the game. The proceeds would go towards the baseball program. Even though this was more or less a mundane task, I naturally did what I was told. Besides, we only had to sell through the first quarter and then we were free to go. As I was biding the time until we could stop I saw a familiar face walking directly towards me. I knew the face very well. It was Sonny Dottolo (Scott's father). Though I was certain he had read the letter that summer, I still didn't think he knew who I was. Moments later Mr. Sonny simply came to me and asked, *"you're Ryan Adams...right?...yes sir...well I just wanted to thank you. You will never know how much your letter meant to my family"*. *"It's no problem"*, I believe was as creative of a response that I could think of at the time. I didn't know what to say or what I should have said. I felt a deep appreciation for him to come and talk to me. Though it might not have been suggested by my facial expression, there was a huge smile on my heart. Mr. Sonny had reassured me that he would be following us this upcoming season, shook my hand, and walked away. He had been the only family member that I talked to during the first semester. He wouldn't be the last.

XII
In every season there are changes

The magic of my junior season had ceased throughout the summer. I was no longer one of the statistical leaders of St. Paul's baseball. I thoroughly struggled in my batting. It was like I was in quick sand. The harder I tried to overcome my slump, the deeper I went and the lower my batting average went. As my struggles became a regular occurrence, I was removed from the two-hole in the batting order. As any person who had a taste of success, I was reluctant to relinquish my place in the spotlight. I took exception that I was no longer batting in the top of the line-up. At first, I thought that it was only a momentary slump and that I would be back to form for the start of the season. It wasn't to be. I was back to putting some undue pressure on myself to perform. I wanted to play baseball at the next level. I think the reality that my abilities may not be college bound stayed in the back of my mind. Ryan Adams was not playing well. The rest of the team was. It seemed that possibly I was the equivalent of a 'one-hit wonder' and I had no idea how to recover.

Even before the beginning of the season, we had reason to believe that we could win the state championship. We were one of the final four teams the previous year and we were bringing almost everyone back. We graduated only one senior (Mathew; our first baseman) yet we gained a move-in senior (Eric; a first baseman). There was more than a belief that we could be the first in St. Paul's history to reach the top of the mountain. I had been one of the leaders of the team as a junior. That role had been legitimate as I was able to back up my 'rah-rah' attitude with performance on the field. As tedious as it had been to reach that legitimacy, it seemed to fade in a manner of moments. Rather, it had faded in about 8 seconds.

Throughout my senior year of baseball, I had become distracted with all that there was in being a senior in high school. I became engulfed in my college choice. I was born and raised an Alabama fan. It had seemed predetermined that the University of Alabama was my future. My grandfather was an Ole Miss graduate and I wanted to visit the campus before I made my decision. When we visited the summer before senior year, I had fallen in love with the campus. Dad saw the look on my face and he was convinced that his vision of both of his children graduating from Tuscaloosa had diminished. It had been an ordeal the entire fall. I had chosen Ole Miss over Alabama but changed my mind around Christmas time (which to this day is still among the best Christmas gifts my dad had received). The choice, though a relief, also meant that playing baseball after the next few months was not likely. It was a tough pill to swallow.

The distractions that occurred during senior year were also very personal. The friendship between Morgan and I had begun to deteriorate to the point that Coach Mauldin talked to us separately about fixing things. Morgan had been more than just a best friend to me throughout high school. He was like my brother. He had been a constant in my life. Part of the uniqueness of my high school experience was that a lot of the friends from either Bogalusa or from St. Paul's never knew of each other. They didn't know the other part of my life. Morgan Strain was the exception to the rule. As long as Morgue was with me, I was never entirely alone. It had come to the point that we didn't even speak to each other. It affected us both. We (Coach Mauldin and I) both knew that I was one of those players that didn't let go of things that happened off the field. Things had affected my game. Even worse, it had affected my attitude. In fact, during the season there had been the only time in our tenure together that Coach Mauldin ever yelled at me after a ballgame.

We played a mid-week game against John Curtis high school out of New Orleans. John Curtis is historically known as a football powerhouse in the state of Louisiana but they were certainly no slouch in baseball either. I had ended our contest the year before against Curtis with a game-ending single in an extra inning affair. This game matched two solid programs that promised to be a quality game.

As a team we had prided ourselves on our ability to lay down drag bunts for base hits. Coach would routinely signal to us to attempt one whenever the defensive alignment allowed. Usually that meant for the third basemen to be playing deeper than normal. Utilizing a drag bunt was also a good way for someone to get out of a slump, which I had been in for the majority of the season.

In the fourth inning of the game Coach Mauldin signaled to me that the third baseman was indeed playing far enough back for a bunt attempt. To put it simply, I ignored the offer. I wanted to swing away. The result was not a positive one and Coach was biding his time to let me know how he felt. His feelings were compounded when we were on the losing end of the game.

After each game we would gather for a prayer and any type of post-game discussion that Coach wanted to have with us. Immediately following the prayer Coach Mauldin looked directly at me and said that I was selfish. I had played as if I was more important than the team. He was trying to help me out; to do what was best for the team in a crucial part of the game and I ignored him. The next day he called me into his office to emphasize how disappointed he was in me. Coach was right. Something had been off. I was lacking motivation. I was lacking inspiration. I needed to refocus and time was running out on the season.

As the season progressed we were no match statistically for the team that stood on the same field just one year prior. We broke the homerun record in 1998 with twelve as a team. We ended 1999 with forty-three as a team. In 1998 we willed ourselves to the district championship. In 1999, though, we came up just short. One of my biggest strengths and, consequently, biggest detriment is that I take things personally. I felt that if I had maintained my focus, we would have repeated as district champs. I was responsible for doing my part for the betterment of the team. Now, the final countdown of my senior season was nearing. The last at-bat I would ever have was coming up. As the slogan had been for the team when I was a sophomore, it was 'now or never'. Anything that had transpired up to that point was done. The other seniors and I still had a choice as to how we were going to be remembered. The season, our careers together, and this journey were going to come to an end. We still could determine the terms to that end. Then, we entered the playoffs.

Blinded by the fact

Something is always desired in life
by those who cannot comprehend what they already have
They live their lives as it is an open book
Yet their understanding doesn't go any farther beyond the cover
These poor souls view their lives in the un-shuffled deck,
Not the dealer
Blinded by the fact that their placement has already been dealt with
Blinded by the fact that what they have
is more than what they actually need
Blinded by the fact that the cover
Is one step closer to the end

October 1998

XIII
I play to go out a champion

Despite our second place finish we were surprised to find that we were given the number one ranking in the state in our classification. We had to win five games in a row if we wanted to win it all. The ranking insured nothing. We were not going to intimidate any of our opponents. We were, though, more focused than ever before. I was more focused than ever before. The absence of my best friend had ended and I was alright with how my final weeks as a St. Paul's student had gone (seniors were done with school prior to the beginning of the playoffs). I was playing like I done as a junior. There was something about the spotlight of the playoffs and the notion that I may not play after this. I liked this type of pressure. I had gained the familiar perspective that I had the previous season. I was having fun just playing baseball. If this was going to be the last time I was going to play baseball, I had no intentions of losing.

In the first round of the playoffs we had to travel to Lake Charles to play Sam Houston High School. Their fans put speakers right behind our dugout in hopes of making us nervous. It was no use. We scored more than ten runs in the first few innings. When we were beginning to think that the game was all but over, Houston mounted its comeback. The game ended a lot closer than it maybe should have been but we had secured round one on the road. The nature of that first round made me wonder if we really had a shot. I was not in doubt as whether or not we could win it all but up to that point, I hadn't even thought of what would happen if we lost. This would be one of the last times I would have this thought.

It was the day before the second round baseball game and I was getting a few swings in the cage. After finishing my round, the question that I heard twice now came from over my left shoulder. *"Excuse me…you're Ryan Adams right"*? As I turned I saw the face of Scott's oldest brother Peter. It had been nearly ten months since I sent the letter but he wanted to repeat the same sentiments that his father had. *"Ryan, it's nice to finally meet you… I'm Peter"*. I knew who Peter was; his brother had looked just like him. He wanted to tell me, again, how much that letter meant to him and his family. He said they were pulling for us. They were pulling for me. With a grin I shook Peter's hand and just knew how the game the next day was going to end. I had been given yet another reminder of what was going on here. It was not a matter of if. It was only a matter of time.

We successfully made it through the second and third rounds of the playoffs. Again in the semifinals, we were now to face probably the toughest opponent of the tournament in St. Thomas More. Their pitcher was 12-0 on the year and their student section (supposedly very intense) was located right behind me in left field. They said everything they could to get under my skin. The result of their banter was me having the best game of my career: a rally starting double and the game winning hit. We managed to add another run afterwards and we achieved what no other team in the program's history had before. We won the semi-finals with a dramatic 4-2 victory. We had one game left to go and I was going to be able to end my career where it only felt right to do so; down from the corner of Adams St. and 8th avenue.

Five years of my life was going to culminate in a two day span. On Friday May 15th, 1999 I was going to play my last game ever and the next day I was going to graduate from high school. When I reflected the days prior the state championship, everything had seemed so surreal. It had not happened as I had originally planned. But then again, I was well aware by this point that it had never been about my plan. I was apart of something far greater than myself and it wasn't over yet. There was no coincidence as to when my first home run was going to be. It was not by chance that I had an assignment about mentors soon after Mr. Terry's death. Nothing had been by mere circumstance. The only family member in the Dottolo family I had not met was Mrs. Kathy herself. It was not coincidence that our first official meeting came hours before we played for the state title.

The introduction to Mrs. Kathy was different than the rest. When she approached me she did not confirm who I was. She just said my name and I hers and we gave each other a hug. She told me it was nice to finally meet me and that Scott was with us that day. I knew he was. I knew we would not let him down. The day was ours. There would be only one way for this to end. In front of the 2,000 people at our home field, St. Paul's baseball could become state champions for the first time ever; only Woodlawn High School from Baton Rouge stood in the way.

The game itself was a story all on its own. Unfortunately it was the fastest game that we played all season. I don't think any of us wanted it to end. We controlled the game from beginning to end but that wasn't reflected on the scoreboard. My final at-bat came in the 6th. Though it didn't play into the outcome of the game, the last time I stepped to the plate in high school I hit a double down the left field line. As I reached second I took a moment to point to the student section beyond left field. I knew it was my final time to be on base in that uniform.

Had I scored we would have had increased from our two run lead but, as it was, we entered the 7th inning leading 3-1. Woodlawn tied the game and would have gained the lead if it weren't for a play at home plate for the inning's last out. In the home half of 7th we had men on first and second base with two outs. Eric, our 1st baseman, singled on a 1-2 count to defeat Baton Rouge-Woodlawn by the score 4 to 3. It was all over. We were officially state champions.

After the fans stormed the field and before the celebration had begun, there was not a soul that was not overcome with the excitement of the moment. For Coach it had been his 300th career victory and his son had been the winning pitcher. For the seniors, we had done what we sat out to do. They may forget our names but they can't forget that we were champions. During the trophy presentation, Coach gave me one of the highest honors I think I could have been given. Coach Mauldin had asked me to be one of the two players to accept the state championship trophy. I became the first player in the history of the program to touch it.

There were many meaningful embraces shared that day. I was thrilled by the one I shared with my Mom and Dad. We had been through so much together. Some of the Bogalusa boys arrived to show their support. My hug to them didn't justify what they had given to me since that freshman year. My hug with Coach Mauldin was quite special. I was apart of the group that could give to him what he deserved to receive. After things were calming down a few of us decided to visit the fans in the outfield. I ran towards left field to high five some of the people on the other side of the fence. One of those that I saw was Mrs. Kathy. Unlike before the game, in this encounter, no words were exchanged. It was the last embrace of the day. Through the fence we held hands, looked at each other and with a tear, we smiled. Nothing was said....there didn't need to be. We knew what just happened.

Picture With Bogalusa Boys

Last At-Bat

Post Game Celebration

XIV
...And for the love of the game

It was seemingly a fitting end. I came into high school as the quiet kid afraid of what to say. I left as a kid that had no need for words. My high school career had come full circle. There is not a moment that I still don't think about those who I lost. I wish that I could have gotten to know Scott better than I did. I think Mr. Terry would have liked to see me coach. I wish Brett could have met my kids. I wish I didn't have to go through what I did but at the same time I would not trade the pain that I felt with anyone. That was my pain. This was my journey. I am convinced it is what I had to go through to become who I am.

In the years that have followed the events of high school, I have certainly developed as a person. This story, though, has been what I always seem to revert back to in any decision that I make. I have trusted in my faith for everything to work out as they are supposed to.

The book title and poem was written in the summer of 2000. I had just begun a job and scholarship opportunity as the manager for the University of Alabama baseball program. It was a position that I hated but necessary to do if I was to ever to be a good baseball coach. Sitting on the porch of my apartment, I just wrote and with one revision, "To Be The King of Diamonds" developed. I had no intention of ever saying this poem to anyone. Honestly, how often does poetry come up in everyday conversation? It just so happened that an opportunity would arrive. At the team Christmas party everyone was given a chance to say why they were at Alabama and what they were looking forward to for the season. I happened to be last to speak. I used the opportunity to say that they all knew that I did not like being a manager and in regards to why I was there…I told them my poem. It was said aloud in front of the college baseball team that I had dreamed of being apart of but wasn't good enough to play for. It was the first time that I ever said it to a group and it was well received. With this instance, my post-high school journey had begun.

When I graduated from Alabama there were not as many teaching jobs available as I thought. Schools were hiring first-year social studies teachers. They just weren't hiring me. I received seven rejections in my search for my first job. My focus had been to stay in Alabama or move to Georgia. I had no intention of moving back to Louisiana. I did, however, apply at St. Paul's. After months of lulling over rejections, it was my alma mater that hired me. Two days prior to receiving the offer, though, I met a girl. Before I could sign my contract with St. Paul's, the principal from Chelsea, Alabama called to see if I wanted to interview. A week later I called St. Paul's to inform them that another opportunity arose. Five days later I was offered the position at Chelsea High School. More importantly, eight days into the eighth month after I met her, I was engaged to the love of my life.

Finally, after spending five years teaching and coaching at Chelsea High School, it was time for me to move on with my career.

Coach Mauldin and I had remained close ever since I graduated as one of his players. He had retired from coaching a year after my last game. The semester after into my job at Chelsea, coach came out of retirement and accepted the head baseball vacancy at Northshore High School in Slidell, Louisiana. Each year I would come to visit and hear his sales pitch about coming back home. I had no intention of ever coming back. Until one day, I did. I wanted to work alongside my former coach. It was a Monday in March 2009 that I received the phone call to offer me the job to come back home. The next day it became official. That date was March 17th.

My experiences had given me a life. I have come to believe that everything happens for a reason. Could I have played baseball beyond high school if I had only played the game for the fun of it?... probably. Would I have been better off handling my emotions had I just relaxed and been myself?...I'm sure I would have been. Could I have avoided the confrontations in the batting cage? Could I have been bound for a more financially lucrative career?...maybe so. But it wasn't to be. And I don't think it should have been. Had things happened differently, I would not have met my wife Melanie. I wouldn't have my two beautiful children Sadie and Walter Lee. I wouldn't have spent my college career rededicating myself to baseball and wanting to be a coach. I wouldn't have found my way to Chelsea, Alabama and taught the students that convinced me to write a book. I wouldn't have gotten the opportunity to return to Louisiana to coach alongside Coach Mauldin.

I believe that everything works out the way it should. It was necessary for me to experience things the way that I did. In my journal entries I had classified my moments in simple terms. Every success for a cowboy is defined as to how he does within 8 seconds and (since my jersey number was 8) I would as well. How did I come to be a teacher and a coach? My answer is simple: a speech, a homerun, and a letter. That is what it took to create my state of mind; it took my 'eight' to be the king of diamonds. For that, I have found my purpose in life and I am grateful.

State, Of Mind

Down from the corner of Adams and 8th
I wished to be among the best in the state,
Of mind if it mattered to them what I brought
The life they never knew or the battles I fought
The footsteps I left would be erased in time
But still there were few who knew they were mine
As this chapter of the book came to an end
Another would start and I would ascend
To a better me I could begin to create
To accommodate change I would also my state,
Of mind if it matters to those I'm around
What I've learned from life and what I have found
But in a brave new world what could I do
For things from the soul are much harder to prove
And I've seen a strong bond with people and fame
For one is much more effective when they notice your name
Still I wish that this was or could be my fate
Well maybe its not, but still it my state,
Of mind that it matters more so to thee
Not the ones that I changed but the ones who changed me
From the sparkles and fades to how I have grown
Could be part of the footsteps now edged in stone
When the finale should come to what I've begun
Mind you it matters not the outcome, because I've already won
Never perfect will I be or always right will I choose
But a better person am I from what I've gone through
Should still waters turn rapid and there not be chance to remind
Remember forever, for always they're kept in this state of mine

July 2002

85

Coaching Picture

Melanie and I

Dad, Morgan, and I

Afterword

Even as an educator, I will always be a student. The road that has taken me to this point in my life has taught me so many lessons. However, I am now understanding (and thankful) of the fact that there are still more lessons to be learned. I never reached the boyhood dream of playing college baseball. But I received something much more from the game that few could match. When I entered into college I had no intention of becoming a teacher. But I know now that it was what I was supposed to do. I do not always love being a teacher. As any job, it can be tedious at times. But I do love what I do for a living.

I have been given the gift of talking to young people and letting them into my world; breaking down the walls of lesson plans and curriculum and teaching things the only way I know how. In my reflections of my teenage experience in the classroom, I struggle to recall many of the facts, notes, or test scores. I do, though, remember that speech. I can not recollect the outcome of every game that I played. I do, though, thoroughly embrace the means that Coach Mauldin used to develop me as a man. My students may not be able to recite all of the information from my class. But they remember the day they heard the story.

In each class period I attempt to do something that will put a smile on a kid's face. Whether it a subtle joke or a few words, I always want to them to leave the room a little happier than when they arrived. With the routines of a school day, of course, this does not always happen. I have been surprised (even though by now I probably shouldn't be) at the times that it does. Most conversation is nonverbal so I can get a general idea as to whether I am getting across to some students by their facial expressions. It is the others (the ones who were like me in high school) that grant me these surprises. Ironically, I have received letters from students giving me a general 'thank you' or expressing how the timing of the story caught them at a time when it was much needed. Some have brought me to tears. You never know how far a few words will go. Scott Dottolo taught me that.

Whether in a classroom or in a workplace, each person you come in contact with has a story. We carry our situations as badges of honor or we hide them to avoid drawing attention to our misfortunes. We all have some type of baggage that we bring. The audience of a teenage classroom magnifies the baggage. Some students that have heard this story can relate to the idea of loss. Some had trials that were far worse than mine. Some just seem to appreciate the pleasant nature of their background. All are alright. I hope that each teenager does not (whether good or bad) forget the lessons of their past. I hope they embrace their experiences. Never forget. Brett Baughman taught me that.

There has not been one instance in which I have told this story that I do not show emotion. I have cried every time. I am unashamed of this. As a coach I am a hugger. I have no issue in disciplining a player or being honest when they are not playing up to par, but I also have no issue in letting them know how much I care about them. I never want to people to ever doubt if I cared. The only way I know how to approach my job is to not hide behind smoke and mirrors. For better or worse, I am the way I am. Everyone can appreciate being told or shown that someone else cares about them. Terry Wood taught me that.

This story has, thus far, been told to roughly 1,000 high school students. I do it, as aforementioned, because I made a promise to myself that I would. The first time I was reluctant as to how it would be received. The reactions were (and have been) overwhelming. At the beginning of the 2007-08 school year, I received one of the highest honors in my few years as a teacher. Chelsea High School has a tradition of dedicating the yearbook to someone. Typically, it has been given to a teacher who is retiring or has had a lengthy service in the profession. In an announcement over the campus television, they announced the dedication to me. The excerpt reads:

Mr. Ryan Adams
Since Coach Adams joined our family 3 years ago, he has been dedicated to his job and to his students. Needless to say, in those few years he has made a lasting impact on the faculty and students here at Chelsea High School...He may not know it, or at least he won't admit it, but Coach Adams has touched and redefined the lives of all of the students he has come across. For this reason and many others the yearbook staff unanimously selected Mr. Ryan Adams for the 2006-2007 dedication.

When I announced in 2009 to my students that I desired to return home to Louisiana, they left me a request. You should write a book. The lessons and memories of Scott, Brett, and Mr. Terry have transcended to the lives of my students. What I am doing is providing something of meaning. My students have taught me that.

I often tell people that I still don't know what I want to do when I grow up. I don't doubt the direction my life took or the direction it is taking. I, as anyone, could play the 'what-if' game. It wouldn't matter. It led me to here. I have been blessed with opportunity. Each time that I have prayed as to whether I can make a difference, I get a question in return. Why not me? God has taught me that. It's the only 8 seconds I'll need.

Acknowledgements

There has been a sense of reluctance for me to write this book. It is something that I have wanted to do for a very long time but never thought it would ever come to fruition. My reluctance has come from how it would be received. The first time I told the story in my classroom, I was uneasy as to how a classroom of high school students would handle it. I have been moved by the reactions that I have received over the years. After the book was first completed, it sat at my home because I knew of the two major hurdles I would have to do before I ever sought publication.

The first hurdle was to receive permission from the Baughman and Dottolo families. Their blessings have been my gift. I would never have pursued this without their support. When each of them read the copy that I sent, it did give them an understanding that their sons are still alive in the hearts and minds of my audience. Until now, the audience had been confined to the walls of my classrooms. Mom had mentioned to me that, in a way, I have become closer to Brett, Mr. Terry, and Scott more after their deaths that I had before. I had never thought of it in that manner but she is right. I am closer to them now and I never knew the entirety of their stories. But I know the lessons they taught me and I hope they are each able to look down with a smile on their faces.

The other hurdle was to show the true meaning of this story... and not through my eyes. I know what telling this story has meant to me. However, it has been through the responses of my students and everyone who has listened or read this that has assured me that I am doing the right thing. The value of the lessons taught to me, from my experiences, have increased merely because they have made an imprint on the lives of some of the young men and women have been blessed to come in contact with. It is not coincidence that my path has crossed with some of these amazing personalities. They have kept this story alive and I wanted their voices to be a part of this book since they were the reason it has been told.

I remember sitting in 10th grade US History the day Coach Adams told this story to the class. It didn't occur to me at the time that being his first year teaching, we were technically the first class to really hear this story, but I know it all started with him holding a baseball. I remember hearing the whole thing and tearing up several times, partly because he was tearing up and partly because of the impact it had on me as a student. I always knew Coach Adams was a caring teacher to each and every one of his students, but to be so vulnerable in front of a class and to share something that meant so much to him as a person went to a whole new level. I can honestly say that when I left the classroom that day, the little wheels in my head were turning a little faster than any other day I had spent in that class. I know it affected everyone differently, and I know that there are many lessons to be taken from his story. But personally, I learned to never hesititate to say kind words because you never know how far they can go and that letting it be known that you care about someone is never a bad thing; everyone wants to be loved. I wasn't aware that he told every class after us this story, but I was glad he made the decision to do so. Throughout the remaining years of high school, Coach Adams was my constant. He was the one teacher that I or any student could talk to because we knew he genuinely cared. I am now 21 years old and have three years of college completed; to this day, I have not been blessed with a teacher or professor to impact me in such a way that Coach Adams has. And I know from talking with fellow classmates that it wasn't just me; he has impacted (and will continue to impact) many more students than he will ever know, simply by sharing his story.

Jena Alfree
Chelsea High School
Class of 2007

I met Coach Adams for the first time my sophomore summer. Not knowing much about him, I learned day by day. I couldn't wait for the second semester to come and the start of baseball season. I would soon come to realize that it was Coach Adams' class that would make my second semester. As each day went on I learned more and more about him, until one day he made an announcement in class that in two weeks, on March 17th, he was going to be telling a story. Two weeks went by and as luck would have it, I had missed that day of school. From there on out that is all I heard from my friends, as to how great the story was. It just added to the suspension of hearing it. I didn't think I was ever going to hear it, I mean, the season had come and gone and the summer was here. With all the pitching lessons I was taking with Coach Adams it really gave us some one on one time to get closer. Finally a day came where he gave me the opportunity to take the day off from pitching. I was able to sit down and listen to the infamous "story". I never would have guessed what was coming next. Words can't describe the feelings that were running through me. It hit me on a physical, mental, and emotional level. Not to mention the respect that was growing every second that the story went on. I can't even start to imagine going through some of the things my coach went through, and yes I do say "my" coach. There isn't anyone that I would rather be coaching me. It's a great feeling to know there is someone out there that wants the same amount of success for me as I do. I trust Coach Adams to insure me with the best of his knowledge. I am thankful for everything to this point and thankful for what is to come.

Shane McKinley
Northshore High School
Class of 2012

As a sophomore in high school, most students have a very small view of the world. In my case, I had lived in this a safe bubble in the small town world of Chelsea, Alabama. Like most other teenagers, I felt invincible. That year, along with about six hundred other students, I got quite a wake up call. After losing a classmate in a car accident, we all struggled as to why this would happen and how to move on after the fact. My junior year, I had the privilege of having Coach Adams as a teacher. In his class, as he had in every class before, he shared a very personal story about some difficult things he had been through in his life. Just as we had a year earlier, he too had lost not one, but two friends. Instead of being angry and sulking about what had happened, Coach Adams had used what he had been through as motivation to be the best he could be. He had taken what was a very sad situation and turned it into something ultimately positive. We can never predict what will happen in our lives, and we will certainly never understand why; all we have control over is how we respond.

Rachel Smith
Chelsea High School
Class of 2007

The first time I ever heard Coach Adams tell his story, I was a senior in high school. I can remember as a junior hearing about the story from all the seniors that had his class, and couldn't wait till the next year when it was my chance. He told the story the Friday before spring break. When 6th period came around there was not a soul in class that arrived late. The room was completely silent as we patiently awaited the start of the story. As the story went on you could look around the room and all eyes were on coach. As the story progressed you could tell how it was starting to effect people. I could see tears roll down some of my classmates' eyes and you could tell that no one thought about anything else but what was going to come next. This was one of the greatest and most helpful stories I have ever heard and read. After hearing Coach Adams' story it made me realize that up to a point we had lived similar lives. I wasn't always the best player in baseball but I always tried my best to be as good as I could. Hearing his story hit home with me. On the day I heard the story we had a baseball game. Just like him I wasn't a homerun threat. That day at the game I hit my first home. After I watched it go over, I looked over to first base and I pointed at coach as I rounded the bag telling him that one was for him. It was one of those "8 seconds" that I would never forget. This story is what changed my mind about a lot of things in life and taught me a lot about people. The one thing I took from the story is that no matter how bad things can get sometimes, sometimes you must keep going and pushing hard through life to become the person you want to become. Ever since Coach Adams allowed me to review the story for him, I have read it every couple of months to help me remember the day I heard it the first time. I know whoever hears it from now on will only be the better for it.

Stephen Icolano
Chelsea High School
Class of 2008

I first heard Coach Adams' story when I was a sophomore in high school. As a sophomore in high school you don't really know who you are, who you want to be, or what you want to do with your life. All you really want to do is fit in. Listening to Coach Adams talk about his journey taught me that you don't have to know any of those answers just yet. It taught me that who you end up being is a product of the decisions you make, and the experiences you go through. Coach Adams is not the person he was at the beginning of his journey. Likewise, who I was the day I heard his story is not who I am now. Today I can look back and understand from his story that life is completely unpredictable, and all we can do is dedicate ourselves to the things we love

and work hard to be the best at what we do.

Sally McCoy
Chelsea High School
Class of 2007

Each note or comments ever received concerning this story are very dear to me. The following entry is a little bit different from the rest. Though the message is similar to the others, the manner in which this letter was received makes it unique (and a fitting end to these pages). I had wanted my last lesson at Chelsea High to be memorable. That day had been the first time I brought my original journal into my classroom. My last lesson was about "the proper good-bye". I mentioned that life is a series of quick endings. Your mind builds momentum for occasions and when they are over there seems to be a feeling that something went unfinished; that something went unsaid. Our lives are a collection of "8 seconds". It is not often that we are able to control how things end. We are not able to give the proper good-bye.

Two months into my new job at Northshore, there was a note delivered into my school mail-box. The note was from a former Chelsea student that had been much like I was in the classroom. She was quiet and reserved. There were only few occasions in which she and I had exchanged words. Her letter, however, spoke volumes. The following are her comments:

Dear Coach,
I wanted to thank you for sharing your story with us. As a writer, I crave stories and as an inquisitive person, I crave to know people beneath the surface. You have impacted me in a way, I'm quite sure, are unaware of. My older brother is the same age as you. He is a coach and a history teacher and relates to his students a lot like you do. Last year, he and his wife went to be teachers in Taiwan. It has been extremely hard not to be around him, but having you as a teacher has helped me not miss him as much. I have dealt with loss all my life, and though it wasn't anyone dying, I could relate to a lot of things you said

99

*in the story, such as, not being able to talk to anyone. Your
story was inspiring and helped me think through and process
all that has happened to me. It helped with all the things I
tried to hide deep inside and just forget. I pray that one day
my story will help people like your helped me. I wish I could
have known you better. I have always been okay with letting
other people talk. It was never important for me to have all
the attention in school. I know it is alright just to be the way
that I am. I wish you all the best and I am content, now, in
saying good-bye this way.*

Rebecca Simpson
Chelsea High School
Class of 2009